A Critical Analysis of Vijay Tendulkar's

Silence ! The Court is in Session

Dr. Beena A. Mahida

CANADIAN
Academic Publishing

2014

Price : $27.86

First Edition : December, 2014

ISBN :   978-1-926488-14-1

ISBN Allotment Agency : Library and Archives Canada (Govt. of Canada)

Published & Printed by
Canadian Academic Publishing
81, Woodlot Crescent,
Etobicoke,
Toronto, Ontario, Canada.
Postal Code- M9W 6T3
Phone- +1 (647) 633 9712
http://www.canadapublish.com

PREFACE

Indian Drama has undergone various metamorphoses after independence Drama in regional Language are still popular in the midst of Multiplexes, because it is a means of spreading morality and entertainment. After all it is one of the branches of Fine Arts Which gives pleasure as well reflects life in its various shades. In regional drama the contemporary Indian Dramatists Mohan Rakesh, Girish Karnard and Badal Sircar are well known in Marathi Drama Late Vijay Tendulkar is ranked as a Frontline Playwright in the Contemporary Indian Theatre.

Drama in India has a long history and in regional languages it is as popular as other literary genres – fiction and poetry. In Indian Literature, drama in English has not attained much popularity because plays in regional languages dominate the theatre. In recent times, Plays in the regional languages are translated in to English and such translations have established link between East and West, and North and South as well as harmony and unity in modern India.

In this context Vijay Tendulkar's Marathi Plays occupy a unique place. When I read the English translation of Tendulkar's plays I decided to pursue my research on plays of Tendulkar and in this decision Dr.R.K.Madalia of the Department of English provided much needed help by accepting to become my Supervisor for the research. He suggested to carry out my research on Tendulkar's major 6 (six) plays and to analyse them from the point of view of characterization, themes and dramatic techniques. Each of the plays of Tendulkar presented new perspective which made stimulating reading.

Tendulkar has not contributed to the modern Marathi theatre but has given it a new dimension. His plays disturb the audience by raising complex issues that remain unsettled even today in modern India. Tendulkar is not feminist but women are at the center in his plays. He treats his women characters with understanding and compassion against men who are selfish and hypocritical. Most of Tendulkar's Plays are Gyno-Centric Leela Benare, of "Silence the Court is in Session" and Kamala from "Kamala" and, Jyoti from "Kanyadaan" leave lasting impression.

I have tried my level best in analyzing the different aspects of Tendulkar's Plays yet I believe that literature offers vast spectrum and if something is left out in my research, I leave it to future scholars to pursue studies that are more elaborate.

This book is slight modification of the thesis. I have separated each play for a separate book to get wider information regarding the play and the details within and tried to focus in details the themes, characters, and important aspects.

Silence the court is in session was the first major play by Tendulkar which lodged a fierce attack on the ideology of glorification of motherhood. It also laid bare the sexual politics in patriarchal norms of family and gender relations.

The success or failure of any work of art depends upon its appeal – whether that appeal proves to be transitory or everlasting. A work of art with an everlasting appeal always remains eternal. It will not be out of the way or excessive exaggeration if the same thing is said about Tendulkar's plays.

Dr. Beena A. Mahida

CONTENTS

1. INTRODUCTION

Art is inevitable part of human culture. Art is knowledge coupled with emotions. Human interest in art has been eternal and this eternity has made man civilized and cultured. Art is concerned with expression and man expresses himself through any form of art.

In literary criticism art is divided into two types. Fine Arts and other than Fine Arts. The function of fine arts is to afford pleasure while other arts satisfy human needs. Architecture, sculpture, music and poetry are fine arts. Drama is included in Fine arts. Other literary forms find expression in statement but drama finds expression in acting. Compared to other literary forms drama is very close to human life hence it is said "Drama makes the spectators hearts dance" Drama is said to be the mirror of the world because on its small scale the full context of human life is revealed. It is a process that originates in the writer's mind and completes itself when it touches the heart of the spectators. It is a world of make-believe and its roots are in performance.

Drama has always remained a unique means to spread morality and to entertain. Long before movies came into being Indian theatre had been a major source of spreading moral value and entertainment. The remarkable feature is that- in spite of the emergence of the Indian cinema, the Indian theatre has not lost significance.

The Indian cinema with all its advanced techniques, sophisticated cameras and freedom of variety has remained unsuccessful in surpassing the Indian Theatre. No doubt – an actor who works in a cinema gets more money than a player of the stage but- the player of the stage gets more appreciation than the actor on the screen. The camera of a movie allows the compensation of a re-take to the actor whereas for the artist of a theatre no re-take is possible. His work demands more sincerity and higher efficiency which finally bring greater appreciation to him.

The tradition of Indian Drama is very old. It goes back to the Sanskrit Drama of ancient India. India being a large country with diverse cultures and regional languages has various traditions of form and matter, distinct and yet having many common factors of dramaturgy. Modern Indian drama is influenced not only by classical Sanskrit drama or local folk forms but also by western theatre following the establishment of British rule in India.

N. S. Dharan, an eminent writer of Indian writing in English writes "Drama in India has a long history". Girish Karnad says that the earliest extant play in India was written as early as A.D. 200. Dating to the days of Bhasa, Bhavabuti and Kalidasa, drama can boast of a rich and chequered history. The early plays were written in Sanskrit, based on the Vedas and the Upanishads. In fact, the Vedas and the Upanishads have never ceased to be sources of inspiration to man of letters both in India and abroad. Down the centuries, Indian drama has undergone various metamorphoses and it still continues to flourish in all regional languages. In regional languages it enjoys almost an equal status along with two other major literary genres, namely fiction and poetry. In Indian literature drama in English is yet to register an appreciable growth. By and large, plays written in regional languages dominate the Indian theatre. These plays are easily intelligible to the audiences. Actors too can easily improvise in them.

Several regional amateur theatres have also flourished from time to time. In the post-Independence period, performing arts were employed as an effective means of public enlightenment during the First-Five year plan (1951-54). As a result the National school of Drama was established under the directorship Alkhazi. Institutions for training in dramatics were founded in big cities. Drama departments started functioning in several universities. The annual Drama Festival was started in New Delhi by the Sangit Natak Akademi in 1954. With so much encouragement coming from so many quarters, drama began to flourish in the regional languages.

During the last few years, several plays, originally written in the regional languages, have been translated into English. Today, a sizeable number of such plays do exist. According to many academicians, it is necessary to incorporate these translations into the corpus of Indian English Literature as they also contribute an important component to it. Such translations of plays have forged an effective link between the East and the West the North and the South of India and contributed, in no small measure, to the growing harmony and richness of contemporary creative consciousness.

According to **Indranath Chaudhary**, when the sahitya Akademi was set up in 1954, Dr. S. Radhakrishnan spelt out its objective as the promotion of the unity of Indian literature, despite India's geographical, political, Social, and Linguistic diversities. Dr. Radhakrishnan gave a slogan to the Akademi that Indian literature is one, though written in many languages. It is in this context that the plays of Girish Karnad in Kannada, Mohan Rakesh in Hindi, Badal Sircar in Bengali and Vijay Tendulkar in Marathi occupy a unique place as pointed out by **Arundhati Banerjee** :

"In the 1960s four dramatisls from different regions of India writing in their own regional languages were said to have ushered modernity in to the sphere of Indian drama and theatre. They were Mohan Rakesh in Hindi, Badal Sircar in Bengali and Vijay Tendulkar in Marathi and Girish Karnad in Kannada.

Rakesh's untimely death left his life's work incomplete, and Karnad has written only intermittently. Sircar, of course, has been almost as active as Tendulkar though his plays can be divided in to three distinct periods. Tendulkar, however, has not only been the most productive but has also introduced the greatest variations in his dramatic creations."

V. B. Deshpande rightly states, "Since the Independence – since 1950, to be precise – the name of Vijay Tendulkar has been in the forefront of the Marathi drama and stage. His personality both as man and writer is multifaceted. It has often been puzzling and curious with a big question mark on it. In the last 55 years he has written stories, novels, one – act plays, plays for children as well adults. Similarly he has done script6 writing and news paper columns as well. And in all these fields he has created an image of his own. Thus he is a creative writer with a fine sensibility and at the same time a contemplative and controversial dramatist. He has made a mark in the field of journalism also. Because of his highly individual viewpoint and vision of life and because of his personal style of writing he has made a powerful impression in the field of literature and drama, and has given the post-independence, Marathi drama a new idiom. By doing this he has put Marathi drama on the national and international Map."

The same indebtedness is expressed by **Arundhati Banerjee** "Vijay Tendulkar has been in the vanguard of not just Marathi but Indian theatre for almost forty years".He not only pioneered the experimental theatre movement in Marathi but also guided it."

While talking about contemporary Marathi Theatre **Dhyaneshwar Nadkarni** points out,

"Vijay Tendulkar leads the vanguard of the avant garde theatre that developed as a movement separate from the mainstream. Tendulkar and his colleagues were dissatisfied with the decadent professional theatre that characterized the Thirties and Forties. They wanted to give theatre a new form and therefore experimented with all aspects of it including content, acting décor and audience communication."

Chandrasekhar Barve expresses a similar opinion about Tendulkar's contribution to Marathi theatre,

"We can say with certainty that Tendulkar has guided Marathi drama that seemed to have lost its proper track, and has kept leading it for over two decades. His place and importance in this respect shall remain unique in the history of Marathi drama. There may be controversies regarding his greatness but his achievements are beyond question.

He has written 28 full length plays, 24 one-act plays, several middles, articles, editorials and 11 plays for children. In spite of his success in every genre, his versatility as a writer has been overshadowed by his fame as a dramatist since drama has been his forte.

Mr. Barve observes,

"His extra-dramatic writing also reveals his pure taste for drama which tries to capture the different tensions and through them, finds "dramatics" accurately".His one-act plays are more experimental than his full-length plays. Most of them have been translated and produced in major Indian languages and some of them into English.

Vijay Tendulkar was born in **1928** at **Bombay** in **Maharastra**. He was born and brought up in Kandevali, a small lane in Girgaon. A lower middle class community dwelt. There and the males were mostly the shopkeepers and clerks. He was living in a typical chawl, in apartments of one room, kitchen, balcony and common toilets, so Tendulkar's upbringing in a lower middle class community provided him chance to perceive middle class minutely which helped him to portray its different shades on the stage.

His **father Mr. Dhondopant Tendulkar** was a head clerk at a British publishing firm called Longmans Green and company (Now Orient Longman). His **mother Mrs. Susheela Tendulkar** was a housewife. His father was a writer, director and actor of amateur Marathi plays. He didnot join the commercial drama company as formerly a career in the theatre was not honoured. Four years old Tendulkar used to go with his father to the rehearsals so he nurtured love for the theatre from his childhood. Tendulkar himself considers those rehearsals as a kind of "Magic show". Because like magic he saw the living beings change into characters. He saw with wonder the male performing the roles of woman by changing their voice and movements. He didn't have any exposure to other theatre except what his father staged.

Tendulkar had other **brother** named **Raghunath** and **sister Leela**. His two elder sisters died in infancy. He had two younger brothers but- he was the favourite child of his parents. He was sickly child and suffering from cough and asthmatic wheezing. So special care, protection and love were provided to this sickly boy by the parents for fear of losing him if not protected well. He was given the **pet name "Papia"** and above all he was known as a **"Mother's child"** being favourite of his mother. Emotionally he was more attached with his mother than his father. He remembers how his mother used to feed him forcefully.

Due to his unhealthy body the family servant used to take him to school. It was municipal school. As usual it had small dingy rooms with awful toilets and it had no playground and water at times. In the school also special attention was given to him as he belonged to somewhat well to do family. His teachers used to borrow story books from him and by becoming partial they left him alone at the examination. Thus he studied in an average Indian school, which has no basic facilities but he carries those moments in comparison with sophisticated school where he studied later in life. At 9 years of age he attended "Chikisaha samooha", where he found himself totally strange among the sophisticated children and spacious buildings.

Tendulkar surprisingly started his career as a **writer** at a very early stage of life. He wrote stories and essays when he was **6** years of age. His father was a writer, director and actor so creativity was inborn in him. The unpublished work of his father lay at home and little Tendulkar passed his time with books and had read novel and short stories of eminent writers so he grew up in a literary atmosphere. The seed had already been sown in little mind for literature and gradually it took the shape of huge tree.

He had never imagined himself to be a writer in his childhood. As a small child he wanted to be an engine driver or an acrobat in circus and dreamt of wondering from place to place astonishing the crowd by daredevil acts. He used to visit fairs and circus with his father which were like big fairyland for him. So childlike curiosity, interest and amazement surrounded him along with his keen interest in reading. Sunday and vacation had special attraction for him. On Sunday morning his father used to take him to a large bookshop of his friend used to buy books of his choice. In evening his father took him to chowpatty beach and they travelled in train from Charni Road to Colaba which attracted him a lot. During summer vacation the family used to go for Goa or to Port Ratnagiri.

Tendulkar remembers that his father was a strict disciplinarian, impractical, stubborn but an honest man. "To be honest is a disqualification in todays world" and so Mr. Dhondopant Tendulkar never got the honour of being honest and idealist. He never took bribes or extra fees. But he felt proud to be poor and was very much content with life. Due to this the later life of his father was miserable. The elder brother Raghunath quarrelled with him and left the home. His father was against the dowry system and so Tendulkar's sister Leela didn't get married and had to remain single. It seems that the father had never got family love due to certain principles.

Apart from the influence of the father, Raghunath, his brother also played formative influence on Tendulkar. His brother was a follower of Gandhi and Gandhian principles. He used to attend political congress meetings. The father wanted him to be active in studies but he went astray. He wanted to marry Hansa Wadkar which was unbearable for the idealist father and so the family separated from Raghunath and moved to Kolhapur. Tendulkar used to get gifts like pastries, sweets and pen from his brother. He used to go for English movies with his brother. But his brother died miserably due to alchoholic habit.

The later childhood of Tendulkar passed at Kolhapur – a princely state in Maharastra. At Kolhapur he made himself noticeable by his excellence in reciting English poems. When he was **11 years** old, he **wrote** and **directed** and **acted "Maya Bazaar".** This way, the journey of this veteran writer towards performing arts started. At Kolhapur his friend was the son of one prominent playwright named Na vi kulkarni, who shared the same literary interest with Tendulkar. He even worked as a **child artist** in **two Marathi** Films.

As a teenager, at the **age** of **13** the family shifted to Pune and he attended a new school. He believed that he might have completed matriculation but the **Quit India Movement** was in momentum and Tendulkar was one of those who obeyed Gandhi's call to boycott the school. He started taking part in campaign against Britishers and he used to attend the early morning meetings without informing his parents. At the **age** of **14** while attending such meeting, he **was arrested** and the family came to know about Tendulkar's active participation in freedom fighting. Again he attended the school but now he started bunking the classes and developed the habit of spending the monthly fees of the **school** in watching English films. The visuals had a good impact on him. This exposure to the theatre at an early age has had its strong influence on him as a **successful** dramatist. He says in an interview, "As a school boy I had watched the Hollywood films playing in my hometown, not once, but each one over and over again. I still remember the visuals, not the dialogues which I didn't understand. A more conscious education in what the visual could do came when I worked with the Rangayan Theatre group in Bombay, but watching Marcel Marceau from the last seat in the last row was an enthralling experience. Not a single word was uttered, but so much was expressed. After that I wrote mimes for quite a while. I felt the visual had unlimited possibilities, the word was useless. But I am a playwright, words are my tools, I had to use them." Apart from Films he denoted his time at the city library in reading which helped him a lot during his career as a journalist. But his father was disappointed seeing the poor prospect of Tendulkar.

At Pune, Tendulkar found the **Role Model** of his life –
Dinkar BalKrishna Mokashi, a radio mechanic but a good writer.
He led a very simple life and Tendulkar was impressed by his
personality and the informality of his writing style. His other **Role
Model** was **Vishnu Vinayak Bokil,** a teacher and a writer.
Tendulkar liked his light hearted, jovial and exuberant style. He
remembered one incident of the school when Mr. Vinayak asked
the students to look at the names of rank holders of the school on
the board and asked, "Where are those top rankers now? Does
anyone know?"Then he said that the students should pass the exam
as the parents pay the fees but the marks they get were not
everything. He advised them to develop their personality in other
directions also. It worked as a boosting to the teen Tendulkar to
look beyond the school. Later on, as a writer Tendulkar dedicated
one of his book to this school teacher Mr. Vinayak.

At 16, Tendulkar **left the school** for good. He had no
friends and no any communication with his parents. He wanted to
talk! But with whom! He had to talk with himself! And he put all
his dialogues with his own self on paper through various forms-
poems stories, film scripts and at this stage of his life his writing
acquired a conscious motivation.

At the age of **22** he wrote his **First full length original
play "Grihastha"** which flopped like anything and he took an oath
that he would never write a play in life and to his surprise he has
written **28 full length** plays as well as he has been **working
actively** in the theatre world for the last **45 years.**

He always considers himself a writer first and a playwright after words. About his love for writing he writes,

"The point is more than a playwright, I consider myself to be a writermeaning I loved to indulge in the physical process of writing. I enjoy this process even when there is nothing to be said. Give me a piece of paper any paper and pen and I shall write as naturally as a bird flies or a fish swims. Left to myself, I scribble. And I never get tired of writing... Especially when I write in my mother tongue i.e. Marathi. Writing gives me a pleasure which has no substitute. However, tired I am physically or mentally, the moment I pick up the pen and begin running it on a paperany piece of paper I feel good I feel refreshed I feel as if I am born again. Writing by itself is a luxury for me. When I write, I forget myself, I forget my anxieties..."

He has been writing in different roles by using different mediums. He was **journalist**. He had been **sub-editor** and executive editor in journals and assistant editor of a daily. He used to write editorials with the information received from the second hand sources. This filled him with great dissatisfaction. He says,

"It started with my journalistic dissatisfaction but it grew into much bigger proportions in the sense that it became a matter of conscience as a human being. I became restless."

The violence, the oppression and the exploitation in the society that he witnessed made him restless. And journalism could not offer him a viable solution for his mental agitation. But it does shape his dramatic career. **Gowri Ramnarayan**, therefore points out: "With his exposure to Marathi theatre from childhood, and journalistic background Vijay Tendulkar turned contemporary socio-political situations into explosive drama."

His desire was to start a daily newspaper column and he enjoyed **writing a column** for **six months** in 1993, when Babri Masjid was destroyed. And during those six months he didn't write anything but only enjoyed column writing. He well remembered that during his journalistic days he sometimes wrote for astrology column, when the 'official' astrologer did not reach in time and he enjoyed in forecasting bright future for the unknown readers of the column. As a writer he found good fun in playing the **role** of **an astrologer**.

Being versatile he can put himself in any role. During the period of struggle he did **Ghost writing** with full knowledge that his name would not appear and become known to the readers. He took it as a role with its own "character". His inner personality as a writer underwent a natural change to suit the role. Along with his job in a newspaper he started writing short story and play and even Ghost writing for additional income. His writing developed according to the demands of the roles. He also worked as a **Public Relation Officer** in an industry and wrote copy for add-agencies. He **translated** American Books for the united information services and wrote **scripts** for non-descript Government Documentaries. He played different roles in order to earn his livelihood but his writing practice has brought perfection in writing skill.

Vijay Tendulkar, as a sensitive, sensible and responsible citizen, could not quieten his agitated conscience with his journalistic career. So he left journalism when he received Nehru Fellowship for the 1973-75. During this period, he travelled extensively throughout India and saw directly all kinds of violence.

From this experience, he infers:

"Unlike communists I don't think that violence can be eliminated in a classless society, or, for that matter, in any society. The spirit of aggression is something that the human being is born with. Not that it's bad. Without violence man would have turned into a vegetable."So he perceived both the positive and negative faces of violence.

Regarding ideology he says,

"I do not align myself to any political ideology.......I do have my sympathies with the left"He does not subscribe to any ideology in his plays. Nor does he write for commercial purpose. Moreover, in the words of **Mr. Barve,**

"Tendulkar's plays helped to refine Marathi drama that was so far polluted by propaganda for political awakening and social reforms, cheap and vulgar entertainment". Tendulkar does not subscribe to any particular political Ideologies, as they, including Marxism, are unable to understand the complex human situation and to suggest any viable solution to our Hydra-headed problems. Yet he does not lack political awareness.

He says to **Gowri Ramnarayan** in an interview,

"I had a political background, I was involved in the 1942 movement.Journalism developed my political sense, curiosity for instance ....naturally this got in my writing."

He was actively associated with civil liberties movements in Maharashtra. All this shows his great concern for his country and society. He is a realist and refuses to be fooled by romantic concepts of reforms and movements. He exposed the flaws and the inevitable failure of unrealistic reforms and movements in his plays.

Mr. Tendulkar considers himself as an **actor-writer** and himself acted on the stage during his apprentice days in the theatre but did not find it as exciting as writing. He was an actor on the stage of his creative mind. According to him he acts as he writes in his mind he emotes the **lives** of the character as he writes. They are not written words but a total and spontaneous expression of the mind and the personality of the character which includes not only the words but also the eloquent silence in between the words- broken sentences, the subtle emphasis on certain words, even the pitch of the voice, the gestures of the hands. He can 20 visualize the position of the characters on the stage – the total composition of the scene and even the lighting. Thus he acted their speech, behavior patterns and their ways of looking at things. So he believes he can act better than others because he has acted his play out when he wrote the play. **Mr. Tendulkar** was basically **a man of theatre**, which he had inherited from his father and eldest brother. He had a curiosity for this performing art and subconscious and unquenched desire to explore the magic and beauty of this form. His love for the theatre continued as he wrote plays at school, acted in plays, watched it, discussed it and for the last 45 years he was in the world of theatre. He believes that performing art is addictive.

He writes,

"You can learn the "grammar" but art is not mere grammar. It is an expression it provides endless learning by experiments, by committing mistakes."

He remembered that at a very early stage of his life he had developed curiosity for people and consciously noted the speech habits of people, their manners and personal peculiarities. He gives an expression to it in his writing so some of his characters are related to certain living persons. He believed that the creative process is complicated process. The characters would appear in utter chaos till he conceives it. He could never write a play with only idea or theme in mind but he needed character first with him.

He writes,

"I could not proceed to write a play unless I saw my characters as real life people, unless I could see them moving doing things by themselves, unless I heard them emoting, talking to each other, I was never able to begin writing my play only with an idea or a theme in mind. I had to have my characters first with me ...." Thus, they are not puppets but living persons of distinction.

About the structuring of his play he said he had never attended any courses for this skill but he had learnt it by trial and error method which is very costly. He wrote that one has to own money in experimental theatre. No one sponsors the play and by the time the players correct the mistakes they are doing the last show of the play. For him, the Rehearsal Hall had become the learning ground. In absence of theatrical devices the inner mechanism of a play with its positive and negative points were laid open and he learnt a lot from these brain- storming rehearsal sessions. Apart from experimenting in the theatre, watching rehearsals he used to see play every day once, twice or thrice in one day. He did not bother whether the play is good or bad but it helped him in internalizing the techniques of playwriting – especially the structuring of the play.

He learnt a lot by watching films because a film also has to have a structure. Even the **concerts** of **classical music impressed** him though he did not know its grammar but classical music has its strict rules and regulations. The **reading** of **the poems** also supplied him the knowledge about compact structure and a form. The visit to the **Art Galleries** made him aware about the rhythm, form and structure in good painting. Apart from all these **Peter Brook's** Book (Master Craftsman in the art of Theatre) taught him the foremost principles of theatre world that all visual art including the art of the theatre, have one thing in common- The space, and it is the skill of the dramatist that how meaningfully and ingeniously he fills the space.

Arundhati Banerjee says,

"Tendulkar's first major work that set him apart from previous generation Marathi playwrights was *Manus Navache Bel (An Island called Man)* (1955). His dramatic genius was cutout for the newly emerging, experimental Marathi theatre of the time. His direct association with Rangayan at this point of his career and continous interaction with such theatre personalities as Vijaya Mehta, Arvind and Sulabha Despande, Kamalakar Sarang Madhav Vatve and Damoo Kenkre provided new impetus for creative faculties. Thus Manus Navache Bel was closely followed by a spate of plays (1958). *Madhlya Bhinti (The walls Between) Chimnicha Ghar Hota Menacha (Nest of wax) (1958) Mee Jinklo Mee Harlo (I won, I lost) (1963) Kavlanchi Shala (school for crows) (1963) and Sari Ga Sari (Rain o Rain) (1964)* which would chart the course of avant-grade Marathi theatre during the next few years. There seems to be a consistency of theme and treatment in them despite the apparently desperate nature of their subjects. In all these early plays, Tendulkar is concerned with the middle class individual set against the backdrop of a hostile society."

Most of Tendulkar's plays are in the naturalistic writing. However, his Ghashiram Kotwal is in the folk tradition while his last two plays *Niyatioya Bailala (To Hell with Destiny)* and *Safar (The Tour)* emplay fantasy. The play **"Silence! The court is in session"** (1967) made him the centre of a general controversy. He has already been called the angry young man of the Marathi theatre. He was considered a rebel against the established values of a fundamentally orthodox society **Encounter in** Umbugland (1974) is a political allegory (1971) **The Vultures** shocked the conservative sections of Marathi people with its naturalistic display of cupidity, sex, and violence. **Sakharam Binder** (1972) is probably Tendulkar's most intensely naturalistic play and shocked the conservative society even more than **The Vultures**. In **Ghashiram Kotwal** (1972) he moves from the naturalistic writing in to the folk tradition, it explains the power game that are found in Indian politics. **Kamala** (1981) is based on **a** real life incident reported in The Indian Express by Ashwin sarin. Kanyadaan is also one of the controversial play and branded as anti – Dalit play. It actually tries to show how our romantic idealism fails.

He wrote his plays in Marathi, First, he influenced Marathi theatre and guided it. Later, his impact extended to other Indian languages as his plays were translated into them. Tendulkar perceived the realities of the human society without any reconceived notions, reacted to them as a sensitive and sensible human being and wrote about them in his plays as a responsible writer. He never wrote to win a prize or an award.

He says,

"I have written about my own experience and about what I have seen in others around me. I have been true to all this and have not cheated my generation. I did not attempt to simplify matters and issues for the audience when presenting my plays, though that would have been easier occupation. Sometimes my plays jolted society out of its stupor and I was punished. I faced this without regrets. It is an old habit with me to do what I am told not to do. My plays could not have been anything else. They contain my perceptions of society and its value and I cannot write what I do not perceive".

In his plays he deals with the issues of gender inequality, social inequality, power games, self alienation, sex and violence. His characters are very much real. They are neither completely good nor completely bad. He liberated Marathi stage from the tyranny of conventional theatre with its mild doses of social and political satire for purpose of pure entertainment.

Mr. M. Sarat Babu writes,

"Vijay Tendulkar portrays the contemporary society and the predicament of man in it with a special focus on the morbidity in his plays, which remind us of Nietzche's words "the disease called man" and also Freud's description of human civilization as "a universal neurosis". His plays touch almost every aspect of human life in the modern world and share the disillusionment of the post modern intellectuals, however they seem to highlight three major issues : gender, power and violence."

Vijay Tendulkar devoted his life for the world of theatre as he says ,

"What I like about those years is that they made me grow as a human being. And theatre which was my major concern has contributed to this in a big way. It helped me to analyse my own life and the lives of others. It led me to make newer and newer discoveries in the vast realm of the human mind which still defies all available theories and logic. It is like an everintriguing puzzle or a jungle which you can always enter but has no way out..."Such a prolific and versatile writer has been felicitated with many awards and honours like

1. The Maharashtra State Government Award (1956, 1969 and 1973)
2. The Sangeet Natak Akademi Award (1971)
3. The Filmfare Award (script writer) (1980,1983)
4. The Padmabhushan (1984)
5. The Saraswati Samman (1993)
6. The Kalidas Samman (1999)
7. The Maharashtra Gaurav Puraskar (1999)
8. The Jansthan Award (1999)
9. Katha Chudamani Award (2001)

This legendary theatre man passed away on **19th May, 2008**. He was suffering from Myasthenia Gravis, a neuromuscular disease. He died at the age of 80 in a private hospital at Pune where he was hospitalized since 10th April, 2008.Shirish Prayag, Director of Prayag Hospital stated,"At the time of his demise he was extremely calm and quiet. There was an expression of contentment on his face. His face did not reflect any pain."

Mr. Prayag stated that the family members had discussed the possibility of eye donation but it was decided that since Tendulkar had not expressed such a wish it would be improper to do so. Tendulkar who was in Pune, since he was last discharged from hospital had refused to go back to Mumbai."

According to his wish his last rites were performed at the Vaikanth electric crematorium and prominent theatre and film personalities including Mohan Agashe, Satish Alekar, Haider Ali, Amruta Subhash, Amol Palekar and Atul Pethe, university of Pune vice-chanceller Narendra Jadhav paid last tribute to Tendulkar at the crematorium.

> **Condolence Messages on Vijay Tendulkar's DeathPresident Pratibha Patil** said in her condolence message "Vijay Tendulkar was not only an acknowledged figure in Indian literature but also helped Marathi and all of Indian theatre attain recognition at the international level."

> **Prime Minister Manmohan** Singh in a condolence message to Tendulkar's family said, "his strog espousal of women's empowerment and the empowerment of the downtrodden has shaped public consciousness in post independence India."

> **Leader of Opposition L K Advani** also paid glowing tributes to Tendulkar. He said the playwright was an outstanding writer who gave Marathi theatre a national and international profile."His place, many of which were translated into Hindi and other Indian Languages, were both creative and carried a strong social message,"

- **Maharashtra Chief Minister Vilasrao Deshmukh** also condoled the death of eminent playwright Vijay Tendulkar.In his condolence message, Deshmukh said: "The nation has lost the literary genius and dramatist par excellence. With Tendulkar's death an eventful era has come to an end."

- Noted film **director Shyam Benegal** said : "Tendulkar was one of the greatest playwright of Indian theatre in the last 50 years. Tendulkar wrote screenplay of my films "Nishant" and "Manthan". I respected his creativity and admired him as a human being." "He was a senior professional form our field and his contribution to the Indian theatre was immense," Benegal added.

- **Film director Govind Nihlani** said : "Tendulkar brought modernity to Marathi theatre. He pioneered a paradigm shift in the vision of looking at society and reflecting it through theatre and cinema."

- **Bollywood superstar Mr. Amitabh Bachchan** said : " Vijay Tendulkar was a strong and fearless writer and a great mind. I am deeply saddened to hear the news of his passing away." Amitabh was full of admiration for the man who re-wrote many rules of stage writing. "In today's world it is difficult and though to take a committed stand and pursue it. Vijay Tendulkarji did. And that was his strength. At times this stand is the solitary voice of reason often misunderstood but seldom wrong."

> **Amol Palekar said**: "His death is a loss to theatre and literature. wonder whether this losss will ever be recovered. I am glad I could do my share of archiving his entire body of work for the younger generation when my wife Sandhya Gokhale and I organized a Ten Festival in 2006 which went on for a week.

List of Vijay Tendulkar's Works :

One Act :

    Thief Police

    Ratra Ani Itar Ekankika (1957)

    Chitragupta, Aho Chitragupta (1958)

    Ajgar Ani Gandharv (1966)

    Bhekad Ani Itar Ekankika (1969)

    Ekekacha

    Andher Nagari

Collection of Stories :

    Kaachpatre (1957)

    Dwandwa (1961)

    Gane (1966)

    Phulpakharu (1970)

Essays :

       Kovil Unhe (1971)

       Rat Rani (1971)

       Phuge Savanache (1974)

       Ram Prakar (1994)

Children's Plays :

       Ithe Bale Miltat (1960)

       Patlachya Poriche Lageen (1965)

       Chimna Bandhto Bangla (1966)

       Chambhar Chauksiche Natak (1970)

Novels :

       Kadambari

       Katha Eka Vyathechi : Henry James

       Nave Ghar : Nave Ayushya : Grace Jordan

       Prempatre : Henry James

       Aage Barho : G L Letham (1958)

       Gele Te Divas (1958)

       Devanchi Manse

       Amhu Harnhar Nahi: L E Wilder

       Ranphul : S L Arora (1963)

       Chityachya Magawar : W W Tiberg

       Clarke (1957)

Humour :

Karbhareen : Doroothy Von Doren

Biography :

Dayechi Devta : H D Wiloston

To Aamchayasathi Ladhla (Roosevelt) : K O Pear

Film Script (Marathi)

Samana
Sinhasan
Umbartha
Akriet
22 June 1897

Film Script (Hindi)

Nishant
Manthan
Akrosh
Ardha Satya
Aaghat

Play	Original Title	Original Author	Original Language	Institution	Director	First Show	Pub.	Yrs.
Adhe Adhure	Adhe Adhure	Mohan Rakesh	Hindi	Theatre Unit	Satyadev Dube	11th Jan. 1970	Popular	1971
Lincolon Che Akherche Divas	Last Days of Lincolon	Mark Doran	English	-	-	-	Majestic	1964
Lobh Nasava hi Vinanti	Hasty Heart	John Patrick	English	Rangayan	Arvind Deshpande	-	Parchure	-
Tughaluq	Tughaluq	Girish Karnad	Kannda	Avishkar	Arvind Deshpande	17th Aug. 1971	Niklanth	1971
Vasarach Akra	A street Car Named Desire	Tenesse Williams	English	-	-	-	Popular	1966

Dramatic Works

Title	Institute	Director	First Show	Publication
Ghrihasth (The House Holder)	Mumbai marathi Sahitya Sangha, Drama Wing	Damu Kenkare	1955 Exact date not known	-
Sjro,amt (The rich)	Bharatiya vidya bhavan kala kendra	Vijaya Mehta	12th Dec. 1955	1955
Manus navache Bet (An Island Called man)	Lalit kala Kendra	Damu kenkare	28th Oct. 1956	1956
Madhalya Bhinti (Middle Walls)	Best Art Section	Nandkumar Rawate	4th Nov. 1958	1958
Chimanicha Ghar Hota menacha (The Wax House of the Sparrow	Rangmancha	Vijaya Mehta	27th Dec. 1959	1960
Mi Jinkalo (I Won, I lost)	Rangayan	Vijaya Mehta	20th Oct. 1963	1963
Kavlyanchi Shala (School for Crows)	Rangayan	Vijaya Mehta	5th Dec. 1963	1964
Sarga Sari (Drizzle O Drizzle)	Mumbai Marathi Sahitya Sangh, Drama wing	Arvind Deshpande	18th May 1964	1964
Ek Hatti Mulagi (An obstinate Girl)	Kala Vaibhav	Almram Bhende	21th Nov. 1966	1968

Shatata Court Chalu Ahe (Silence! The Court is in Session)	Rangayan	Arivind Deshpande	28th Dec. 1967	1968
Jhala Anant Hanumant	-	Arvind Deshpande	-	1968
Dambdwipacha Mukbala (An Encounter in Umbugland)	Rangayan	Arvind Deshpande	10th Dec. 1969	1974
Gidhade (The Vulture)	Theatre Unit	Shriram lagu	29th May 1970	1971
Ashi Pakhare Yeti (So Come Birds)	Progressive Dramatic Association, Pune	Jabbar Patel	26th Nov. 1970	1970
Sakharam Binder	Welcome theatres	Kamalar Sarang	10th mar. 1972	1972
Bhalya kaka	Natya Mandar	Arvind Deshpande	5th April 1972	1974
Gharate Amuche Chan (Nice is our Nest)	Welcome Theatre	kamalakar Sarang	28th Oct. 1972	1973
Ghashiram Kotwal	Progressive Dramatic Association, Pune	Jabbar Patel	16th Dec. 1972	1973
Baby	nateshwar	Kamalakar Sarang	29th Aug. 1976	1975
Bhai Murarrao	Theatre Academy Pune	Mohan gokhale	13th Sept. 1977	1975

Pahije Jatiche	-	Arvind Deshpande	-	1976
Mitrachi Goshta (A Friend's Story)	Bhumika	Vinay Aapte	15th Aug. 1981	1982
kamala	Kala Rang	kamalakar Sarang	7th Aug. 1981	1982
Kanyadan	INT	Sadashiv Amarapurkar	12th Feb. 1983	1983
Vithala	INT	Sadashiv Amarapurkar	22nd May 1985	1985
Chiranjeev Saubhagya kanshini	Abhishek	Kamalakar Sarang	14th Dec. 1991	-
Safar	Avishkar	Sulbha Deshpande	6th Jan. 1992	-
Niyatichya bailala Ho (To Hell with the Bull of the Fate)	-	-	-	-

2. SILENCE! THE COURT IS IN SESSION: AN OVERVIEW

Silence! The court is in session (1967), the first Tendulkar's play to become part of the New Indian Drama phenomenon of the sixties and the first significant modern Indian play in any language to centre on woman as protagonist and victim. With its production Tendulkar became the center of a general controversy. He had already acquired the epithet of "the angry young man" of Marathi theatre but now he was definitely marked out as a rebel against the established values of fundamentally orthodox society.

The play is the milestone in dramatic career of Vijay Tendulkar and so **Mr. N.S. Dharan** in his article **"Vijay Tendulkar : A unique writer"** writes –

"Vijay Tendulkar's plays can be said to fall into two distinct groups, namely, Pre-silence plays and Post-silence plays. In the plays that Tendulkar wrote prior to Silence! The focus, by and large, is on the sufferings of the middle class man living in an urbanized, industrialized society.....Silence!, however, marks a change in Tendulkar's attitude towards his favourite subject, that is, the middle class man. For the first time in his dramatic career he began to look into the psyche of his subject and focus his attention on the ugliness he detected therein."

Most of Tendulkar's plays have had their original in his own personal experience. Silence! took shape in his mind during the journey he undertook along with his troupe to Vile Parle, a suburb in Bombay. The conversation among the actors and actresses gave him the much needed impetus to write the play.

Leela Benare, the central character of the play possesses a natural lust for life and a spontaneous joie de vivre, who ignores social norms and dictates. Being different from the others she is easily isolated and made the victim of a cruel game cunningly planned by her co–actors. During the course of this so-called "game" which is meaningfully set in the form of a mock-trial, Miss Benare's private life is exposed and publically dissected, revealing her illicit love affair with professor Damle, a married man with a family, which has resulted in her pregnancy. Professor Damle is significantly absent at the trial denoting his total withdrawal of responsibility, either social or moral, for the whole situation into which he had landed Miss Benare. During the trial he is summoned merely as a witness while Benare remains the prime accused as the unwed mother of his illegitimate child. Interestingly, the accusation brought against her at the beginning of the trial – that of infanticide – turns into the verdict at the conclusion.

Vijay Tendulkar, who is known for his concern for burning social problems of Indian society, through this play tries to explore certain issues of contemporary society like-

(1) Disillusionment in search for individuality by a woman

(2) The concept of modern woman V\s traditional woman

(3) Middle class mentality and its pettiness

(4) The degeneration of dramatic activity

3. DISILLUSIONMENT IN SEARCH OF INDIVIDUALITY BY A WOMAN

One **Chinese Proverb** says-

> "If you want to plant a plant,
>
> You must sow seeds.
>
> If you want to plant a tree,
>
> You must plant a plant, But
>
> If you want to plant civilization,
>
> You must plant a woman"

But unfortunately the status of women remains secondary in this world. She is still considered secondary or weaker sex. An Ideal woman is she who confines herself within the four walls of the house and reares up the children and looks after the family. In India, it is believed God dwells, where women are worshipped but she is exploited more due to patriarchy society. In this play Tendulkar tries to explore the world of woman in which a woman,

34

the heroine gives up the role of an ideal woman and behaves according to her own wishes and as usual the society cannot accept her as an individual and she becomes the object of criticism only.

Mr. N. S. Dharan in his article **"Gyno - centrism in silence! The court is in Session"** writes

"Tendulkar though not a self-acknowledged feminist, treats his women characters with understanding and compassion while pitting them against men who are selfish, hypocritical and brutally ambitious." It is significant that most of Tendulkar's plays are Gyno-centric. Moreover, as a playwright, he seems often to be on the side of feminists, for, he projects women as victim of chauvinistic oppression. The male figuring in his art emerge as purile creatures, for he portrays them as embodiments of hypocrisy, selfishness and treachery. Women are portrayed as helpless victims of the conspiracies hatched by men. Thus we find Benare being mercilessly harassed by her own co-actors."

Subha Tiwari in her article **"Silence! The court is in Session. A strong social commentary"** states

"The whole responsibility of morally upright behaviour is bulldozed on women. Men are by nature considered to be willful, wild, childish, innocent and mischievous. Their sins are no sins at all. The society has a very light parental and pampering sort of attitude when it comes to sexual offences of men. In case of women the iron rod gets hot and hotter. No punishment is actually enough for such a woman. There is no respite, no shade and no soothing cushion for a sinning woman. She must be stained and abandoned. Her femininity, her needs, her very existence must be ignored or rather destroyed. She must be cornered and brutally killedboth in physical and psychological senses. This play is about the pathetic position of women in the male dominated Indian world."

Leela Benare is a school teacher who is as sprightly, rebellious and assertive as the heroines of Shakespeare's romantic comedies, as some critics have already observed. She is sexually alive and she needs to fulfill her desires and for that she is not ashamed of her instinct. She is conscientious in her work and commands the love and respect of all her pupils. She is also an enlightened activist being a member of the amateur theatre group called "The sonar Moti Tenement (Bombay) progressive Association". The other members of this amateur theatre are the Kashikars, Balu Rokde, Sukhatme, Ponkshe, Karnik, professor Damle and Rawte, who all belong to the urban middle class of Bombay.

Benare enters the play with her aggressive, even at times mischievously, seductive, streak in evidence – in her initial interaction with Samant the innocent, compassionate observer in the play. As a teacher Benare is proud of herself she says-

"In school, when the first bell rings, my foot's already on the threshold. I haven't heard a single reproach for not being on time these past eight years. Nor about my teaching. I'm never behindhand with my lesson."

She is very popular among the students and so she praises them as she does not find them hypocrites as compared to the lot of teachers. According to her they do not have the blind pride of thinking that they know everything. She thinks that the community of teachers are escapists. They consider themselves intellectuals. They pride on their book learning. But when there is a real life problem, they run away.

Leela Benare possesses a natural lust for life and a spontaneous joie de vivre, as she states

"We should laugh, we should play. We should sing, if we can and if they'll let us, we should dance too. Shouldn't have any false modesty or dignity. Or care for anyone! I mean it, when your life's over, do you think anyone will give you a bit of theirs?"

She firmly believes in this principle and it is not just an ideology for her but she puts it into practice also she says –

"I, Leela Benare, a living woman, I say it from my own experience. Life is not meant for anyone else. It's your own life. It must be. It's a very very important thing. Every moment, every bit of it is precious."

Thus, she is not ready to be imprisoned in the cage prepared by the society for women. She considers herself as an individual and not merely a woman. Like Rousseu she believes "Man is born free, but everywhere he is in chain". And she, as an individual does not want to bind herself in the established conventions of the society. Perhaps due to this search for individuality as a human being she suffers and becomes an object of criticism in the society. She rejects all boundaries \ limitations that are set for a woman. But in her search for individuality she faces only treachery, hypocrisy, shallowness and vanity of the people.

Her journey from a woman to an individual is clearly brought out in the mock trial in the play. Being an actress in an amateur drama- troupe she arrives at one village to perform one drama with other group members. They are going to perform a mock trial in which they will present a case against president Johnson for producing atomic weapons. The play starts in an empty hall and Benare's entry on the stage suggests significance. Her finger gets caught in the bolt and Samant informs her that in this hall the opening door is problematic as while opening the door if the bolt stays out just a little bit, the door gets shut and one is locked up inside the hall and symbolically Benare is also locked up in this hall where her personal life will be tried.

The members of the theatre group arrive – Mr. & Mrs. Kashikar, Sukhatme, Rokde, karnik, Ponkshe but one (minor character) subordinate actor, Rawte is sick so he does not turn up and they decide to take a local man for his role and Samant, the active boy of the village who is in the charge of the hall is selected for the role. Since he has never seen a court, they decide to perform the court seen totally imaginary so that Samant gets acquinted with the procedure of the court. So they all agree for the visual enactment of the imaginary case against someone. Sukhatme proposes that Miss Benare will be the accused and all the members agree. The trial on Miss Benare begins. Mr. Kashikar seats himself on the judge's chair and says –

"Prisoner Miss Benare, under section No 302 of the Indian Penal Code you are accused of the crime of infanticide. Are you guilty or not guity of the aforementioned crime?"

Benare is stunned, at once but suddenly becomes normal and replies "I just got a bit serious to create the right atmosphere. For the court, that's all. Why should I be afraid of a trial like this?"

Miss Benare is very vocal, very open and frank in her attack on male chauvinism and false concepts of masculinity. So to pay her back in the same coin, the actors plan to expose and humiliate her through this trial. She gets into the trap. Once the trial begins, there is no shelter for poor Benare. She is labeled by all dirty adjectives. Her private life is exposed and publicly dissected, revealing her illicit love affair with Prof. Damle, a married man with a family, which has resulted in her pregnancy. Prof. Damle is significantly absent at the trial, denoting his total withdrawal of responsibility-either social or moral for the whole situation into which he has landed Miss Benare. During the trial, he is summoned merely as a witness while Benare remains the prime accused as the unwed mother of his illegitimate child. During the trial Sukhatme tries to present the value of Motherhood by saying- "Woman is a wife for a moment, but a mother for ever"

So it's unfair on Miss Benare"s part to take the life of the delicate bundle of joy she has borne. Mr. Ponkshe is called as the first witness. He is asked about the social status of Miss Benare and he gives ambiguous answer that to the public eye, Miss Benare is unmarried but to the private eye… He is also asked about the moral conduct of Miss Benare and he replies that she runs after men too much Mr. Rokde & Mr. Karnik are called as second witnesses. They are asked whether they have seen Miss Benare in a compromising situation .Rokde replies that once during the time of night, when he went to Prof. Damle's house, Miss Benare was with Mr. Damle He was not allowed to come in the room. It is concluded that Miss Benare's behaviour is certainly suspicious. Even Samant is called as a witness and he gives imaginary answers to the questions which proves to be correct regarding the private life of Miss Benare. He says that once during the night he has seen Miss Benare in Prof. Damle's house and she was crying and saying

"If you abandon me in this condition where shall I go."
and Prof. Damle said

"Where you should go is entirely your problem I feel great sympathy for you But I can do nothing,. I must protect my reputation.

With this clarification, which is totally imaginary, tears flow from Miss. Benare's eyes. She tries to run away from the dock and goes to the doorway and she tries to unbolt it but it is locked from outside. She is trapped symbolically.

Miss Benare is called and she is asked to take an oath but she remains silent. They discuss about her age and unmarried state, the reasons for her preference to remain single. Actually this discussion reflects the contemporary burning issue-the trend to remain single among women; May be a woman wants to maintain her individuality, does not desire to follows others' command or take up the responsibility. It remains a curiosity for all the members that how an educated, well brought up, earning girl like Miss Benare remains unmarried till at the age of thirty four. Mrs. Kashikar satirically remarks that-

That's what happens these days when you get everything without marrying. They just want comfort. They could not care less about responsibility! It's sly new fashion of women earning that makes everything go wrong. That's how promiscuity has spread throughout our society.

Miss Benare never likes to bind herself with the so called rules and regulations established by the society. She, as an individual, behaves as one human being greets another without bothering, about the limitations of sexes. But this very free nature is criticised by the society, No one is ready to accept Miss Benare's new concept of life as Mrs. Kashikar says "Free! Free! she's free all right – in everything! Should there be no limit to how freely a woman can behave with a man? An unmarried woman? No matter how well she knows him? Look how loudly she laughs! How she sings, dances, cracks jokes! And wandering alone with how many men, day in and day out!"

To the orthodox society she should value the limitations of woman's life. Even the two witnesses Rokde and Ponkshe present totally negative picture of Miss Benare. They try to present her as an immoral woman Rokde, informs, Once while coming back from the performance, on the way, during night Miss Benare held his hand but he didnot encourage her. Ponkshe also gives witness about her immoral living, He was invited by Miss Benare in the Udipi Restaurant. There she revealed that she was pregnant, In order to give father's name to her child she wanted to marry Ponkshe. She wanted to bring up the child. It's only for the child she wanted to go on living and get married. She did not criticise the culprit man. Everyone guesses that he must be Prof. Damle. Mr. Karnik also admits that the accused had very bad past. The accused Miss Benare attempted suicide because of disappointment in love with her own maternal uncle, This revelation shocks everyone and they all exclaim "what an immoral relationship!"

Mr. Kashikar says, "Miss Benare is in education field, so such immoral life of a teacher can corrupt the younger mind." Nanasaheb, the chairman of the education society has decided to dismiss such a lady from the job who is pregnant before marriage. Sukhatme pleads for the punishment to Miss Benare and strongly puts forward his argument-

"The woman who is an accused has made a heinous blot on the sacred brow of motherhood – which is purer than heaven itself. For that, any punishment, however great, that the law may give her, will be too mild for her. The character of the accused is appalling. It is bankrupt of morality. Not only that but also her conduct has blackened all social and moral values. The accused is public enemy number one. If such socially destructive tendencies are encouraged to flourish, this country and its culture will be totally destroyed therefore, I say the court must take a very stern, inexorable view of the prisoner's crime without being trapped in any sentiment. The charge against the accused is one of infanticide. But the accused has committed a far more serious crime. I mean unmarried motherhood. Motherhood without marriage has always been considered a very great sin by our religion and our traditions, Moreover, if intention of the accused bringing up the offspring of this unlawful maternity is carried to completion I have a dreadful fear that the very existence of society will be in danger. There will be no such thing as moral values left. Milord, infanticide is a dreadful act. But bringing up the child of an illegal union is certainly more horrifying. If it is encouraged, there will be no such thing as the institution of marriage left. Immorality will flourish. Before our eyes our beautiful dream of a society governed by tradition will crumble into dust...... I make a powerful plea "Na Miss Benare Swatantryamarhati" "Miss Benare is not fit for independence' with the urgent plea that the court should show no mercy to the accused, but give her the greatest and severest punishment for her terrible crime."

So, contemporary Indian society, with its roots grounded firmly in reactionary ideas cannot allow the birth of a child without wedlock. So Benare is accused of immorality, sin, promiscuity, over-sexuality and so on. The situation of Miss Benare suggests that women are to be used, stained forever and then thrown away. The man responsible for it does not have the courage to accept the act. He has performed. He can not bear the responsibility attached to romantic liaisons. The significant presence in the play is the absence of Damle. It is as though the woman has got pregnant all by herself, the male counterpart has no role, no responsibility in the matter.

Against all such charges Miss Benare tries to defend herself and it is represented through her long soliloquy, which has become famous in the history of contemporary Marathi theatre. "It is important to note here that Tendulkar leaves us in doubt as to whether or not Benare at all delivers the soliloquy, thus suggesting that in all probability what she has to say for herself is swallowed up by the silence imposed upon her by the authorities. In fact, during the court proceedings on several occasions, her objections and protestations are drowned by the judge's cry of "Silence!" and the banging of the gavel,. Benare's monologue is reminiscent of Nora's declaration of Independence but lacks the note of protest that characterizes the speech of Ibsen's heroine. It is more a self – justification than an attack on society's hypocrisies. It is poignant and sensitive and highlights, the vulnerability of women in our society.

So, Benare's inner frame stirs a little to communicate to us what she knows about men who profess love but, in fact only hunger for the flesh. She says.

"Yes, I have a lot to say. For so many years. I haven't said a word. Chances came, and chances went. Storms raged, one after another about my throat."

She says the very word "life" gives a pang of joy. To live is life. To sing, to feel to experiment, to enjoy, to dance, to breathe, to travel, to know, to explore – all this is life. But when you do all this, the society labels you as "evil" and gives a verdict that hangs you. This is the paradox of life – to live or not to live.

"Life is like this life is so and so Life is such and such. Life is a book that goes ripping into pieces. Life is a poisonous snake that bites itself. Life is a drudgery. Life is a something that's nothing or a nothing that's something….. Milord life is a dreadful thing. Life must be hanged…. Life is not worthy of life. Hold an inquiry against life. Sack it from its job."

And it signifies that she is disillusioned with life. Through her experiences she has learnt that Only one thing in life is important that is body. She reveals, that the beginning of her exploitation begins with her maternal uncle who had exploited her sexually in her teen age. She confesses that it was a sin but she was helpless. In her strict house, only her maternal uncle was close to her, who used to praise her bloom of youth. She was only 14 and did not understand the ways of the world, In his company she got the whole meaning of life and she insisted on marriage. So that she could enjoy her beautiful dream openly. Her mother too, failed to understand her and support her. The uncle turned tail and ran. She attempted suicide by throwing herself off from the parapet of the house but she did not die. Her body did not die nor did her emotions.

She started her life again, studied and finally settled into a teaching job. As a teacher she comes in contact with Prof. Damle whom she considers quite intelligent, and academically bright. Again she fell in love. This love is intelligent It is not love but it is worship she says –

"It isn't love at all – it's worship! But it was the same mistake. I offered up my body on the altar of my worship. And my intellectual god took the offering and went his way. He didn't want my mind, or my devotion – he didn't care about them! He wasn't a god. He was a man for whom everything was of the body, for the body! That's all again, the body."

It is little wonder that Benare's monologue towards the end of the play is directed against men in general , and professor Damle in particular. Here, she becomes the playwrights mouthpiece.

She is in dilemma whether to hate or to love her body, But she overcomes the dilemma and says where she will go if she rejects body. She should not be ungrateful to her body. It has given her beautiful moments and right now she is carrying within it the witness of that time – A tender little bud. She says-

"My son – my whole existence! I want my body now for him – for him alone. He must have a mother…… a father to call his own – a house – to be looked after – he must have a good name!

After listening to Miss Benare's justification the court pronounces the verdict. Mr. Kashikar gives the judgement that her

46

sin can not be forgiven. It must be expiated. Social customs should be observed and marriage is the very foundation of the stability of society. Motherhood must be sacred and pure and Miss Benare has tried to dynamite all these. She is a teacher and the future of posterity is entrusted to her. The authority of the school has decided to dismiss her from the job and he pronounces the verdict –

"No memento of your sin should remain for future generations therefore this court hereby sentences that you shall live. But the child in your womb shall be destroyed."

Thus, the accusation brought against her at the beginning of the trial that of infanticide- turns into the verdict at the conclusion. Principally because the orthodox Indian society cannot accept the birth of a child born without socially approved marriage.

So the play dramatizes extreme form of powerlessness for a woman. A woman can never live as an Individual. A woman is either "devi" or "devil". A woman who enjoys sex is something odd and dirty. In this patriarchal society, pleasure is considered to be the sole domain of males. The society does not accept women as normal human beings who have vices as well as virtues. Subha Tiwari in her article "Silence! The court is in session : A strong social commentary" writes –

"At a deeper level, the play is a comment on lack of individual importance in life, the meaninglessness of life, and the absurdity of various human situations, In philosophical terms, this play is a blow to all those who seek meaning out of this mundane, bizarre, ordinary human existence. To live is to be "exuberant" and "exuberant" one is not allowed to be. How often we meet parents who teach their children to laugh mildly. Everyone is scared of being wild. And wildness is part and parcel of human nature. Socializing in this sense means living coyly and submissively. Life becomes death. The society compels one to live less and less. It forces one to live not life but death itself. This sort of life gives birth to all sorts of anomalies. We see abnormal people all around with "so sweet" faces but complex pervert's mind as Miss Benare says –

These are the mortal remains of some cultured men of twentieth century. See their faces – how ferocious they look. Their lips are full of lovely worn out phrases! And their bellies are full of unsatisfied desires."

How true these comments are for contemporary men! Every man is a wolf wrapped in the skin of a lamb. He wants his "Pound of flesh" For him every woman is virtually her body – bones, flesh, curves! A woman is not identified with her intellect, her ability, her intelligence, her courage, or knowledge. A woman, whosoever she may be, is just her body. Even women themselves have internalized this vision about themselves. They see their own selves as bodies. That is why they are afraid and ashamed of old age, wrinkles and white hair. They view themselves primarily as sex objects. This is what patriarchy, has done to women – poisoned their self perception beyond repair.

Leela Benare is mercifully different. But difference and deviation are things Indian society does not give to its women. So Leela Benare pays the price of being different."

4. CONCEPT OF MODERN WOMAN VERSUS TRADITIONAL WOMAN

Shanta Gokhale, a senior theatre critic, historian, playwright and director, writes in her article "For Tendulkar, the primary compulsion is and has always been humanistic. Man's fight for survival, the varied moralities by which people live, the social position of women, the covert or overt violence in woman beings, these are his abiding concerns. They appear in his plays in different forms."

Tendulkar has created memorable male and female characters. But it is his women, on account of their unique position in society, who help to reveal his social conscience, and it is they who emerge as the columns and beams on which he builds his structures. In some of his plays, Tendulkar presents women in pairs. They are quite different from each other in behavioral traits, class and character. But underneath these superficial difference lie lives that resemble each other in the ultimate truth of being commanded by men, for their pleasure and under their laws. The best example is Leela Benare and Mrs. Kashikar in "Silence! The court is in session."

Leela Benare is young, single, unconventional, full of laughter, full of pride in her dedication to and skill in teaching and always happy to attack hypocritical facades and watch them crumble. In her view men aren't superior beings by definition. They must prove themselves so before they can command her respect. The man she has had a passionate relationship with and whose child she is carrying is one of the few men she respected for his fine mind and apparent integrity. However, she has now discovered his feet of clay. He does not have the strength to stand by her and own his child. She has made a desperate bid to get one or other of the unattached men in her group to marry her in order to give the coming child a name. Predictably not one has agreed to her proposal. It is in this delicate state of body and mind that she is trapped by her colleagues into being the accused in a mock trial."

Mr. N.S. Dharan writes in **"The Tongue – in cheek in Silence and Kamala"**

"During the session of the entire "mock-trial" Mrs. Kashikar never misses an apportunity to insinuate her venomous comments directed at Benare as she is extremely envious of Benare's boundless independence. Herself, suffering from a persecution complex on account of her barreness, and her abject dependence on her husband. She is utterly spiteful of Benare. In the closing act, Tendulkar gives Mrs. Kashikar ample opportunity to torture Benare with a view to exposing a discontented woman's irrepressible malevolence against a superior, successful being. For instance, she stops Benare getting out of the torture "where do you think you're going? The door's locked! Sit down!

This is a fine instance where Tendulkar satirizes, woman to woman relationship."

Mrs. Kashikar on the other hand is middle aged, married housewife conventional and disapproving of "free women" like Benare. The most important thing about her is that she is childless. She is as much keen as the men to draw blood when Benare is put on trial. She has an obvious problem with Benare. She is the single free woman, the working woman, the one who is vying for equality with men in their own world. Her very existence places a question mark against the emptiness of Mrs.Kashikar's life. That is why she offers her help with such alacrity when the men shy away from physically forcing Benare into the dock. They are all middle class men who must not be seen to harass a woman. Tearing her apart emotionally is perfectly permissible.

Mrs. Kashikar cannot have ever admitted, even to herself, that it is on account of the sacrosanct institution of marriage that she is open to Mr. Kashikar's constant insults and snubs. He has an automatic right to do so by virtue of being a man, Subha Tiwari in her article – "Silence! The court is in session: A strong social commentary" comments

"The duo of this husband – wife reminds one of Mamapapa in Anita Desai's Fasting, Feasting. The couple is a super hypocrite, leading a false life that is devoid of any meaning. Tendulkar brings out the hollowness of their life so well. Mr. Kashikar buys flowers for wife. Mrs. Kashikar buys shirts for husband. They make a constant show of fondness in public. Their perpetual show of love becomes distasteful and repulsive. Mr. Kashikar, a male chauvinist does not let the wife speak at all".

When the group is considering names for the accused in the mock trial they wish to conduct as practice before the real thing, she offers herself. This is how the exchange goes –

Mrs. Kashikar	:	Shall I be the accused?
Mr. Kashikar	:	No (Mrs. Kashikar falls silent) The minute there's half a chance to butt in, you're right there, pushing yourself forward.
Mrs. Kashikar :		(Embarrassed) enough, so I won't be the accused I hope that pleases you.
Sukhatme	:	Let's forget all of you. Kashikar, let's make someone else altogether the accused. That's best. Our Miss Benare will be the accused well Ponkshe, how's that for a choice?
Ponkshe	:	Good enough.
Sukhatme	:	There should be no argument about that,

eh! Mrs. Kashikar?

Mrs. Kashikar :   Fine if you so. And at least will get to see how a trial against a woman is conducted (Turus to Mr. Kashikar by habit). Isn't that right? It's good to see these things.

Mr. Kashikar :   (Sarcastically) oh yes! You'd think they're going to appoint you judge in the supreme court.

Mrs. Kashikar :   That's not what I meant.

Mrs. Kashikar does not take such suppression of her mind and spirit quietly. She mutters angrily. One suspects that, had she had the economic power that Benare has, she might have protested more actively. However, the way things are, there is no choice for her but to be a participant in the patriarchal system. She chooses to be an enthusiastic one because, if she is to retain a shred of self-esteem, the least she must do is to glorify her own state. That is why her testimony against Benare is such a bitter diatribe, but brazenly parading as sociological observation, when she is asked why Miss Benare has remained single till such an "advanced" age, her response is very melicious.

One cannot help feeling a twinge of compassion for this bitter woman who will let down her own kind to establish herself on the right side of man made social codes. Benare on the other hand, has our sympathy from the moment she becomes prey to the group's bloodthirsty instincts despite the fact that neither her sin nor reported behaviour makes her a particularly sympathetic person, she is not a true rebel, for she is not conscious enough of the politics of gender to be that. She is not a true victim because she is not innocent or good-natured enough to command all our sympathy. She is not consistently principled for, on the one hand she is contemptuous of the men of her group and on the other hand she has asked two of them to marry her after her rejection by her lover, Damle. Her reason for, doing so is also oddly conservative. She wants her baby to have a name."

Tendulkar has made Mrs. Kashikar ridiculous and dangerous in an insidious way. But he has also made it possible for us to sympathize with her. He has not idealized Benare, but forces us to sympathize with her. In this way he allows women their foibles and weaknesses without forfeiting any part of the human goodwill he wants us to have towards them.

5. SATIRE ON MIDDLE CLASS MENTALITY AND ITS PETTINESS

Mr. N.S.Dharan rightly states in his paper **"The tongue-in-cheek in Silence! And Kamala"**

"Tendulkar's plays Silence! And Kamala are nothing if not satirical, which direct their barbs mainly against the urban middle class. In Silence! Tendulkar exposes the hypocrisy, selfishness, sham, moral standards and the sadism latent in the immediate colleagues of the buoyant but belligerent Benare.

"The Sonar Moti Tenement (Bombay) progressive Association" an amateur theatre troupe belongs to the urban middle class society of Bombay. This "experimental theatre" has Mr. Kashikar, a self-styled, social reformer, as its chairman. As for the other artists in the troupe, Balu, Rokde is a helpless student, dependent on the kashikars. Sukhatme is a pretentious lawyer, Ponkshe an inter-failed clerk, Karnik an "experimental theatre actor", Benare, a school teacher and Damle a professor. Tendulkar brings them all together under the banner of an amateur theatre, in order to highlight the hypocrisy latent in this microscopic cross-section of the milieux of the metropolitan Bombay middle class.

Benare functions as the central consciousness in Silence! It is mainly through her ironic perception that the audience get an insight into the other character….."

This play exactly describes middle class mentality and its pettiness. The theatre members are a bored, frustrated and repressed lot. The first one is the president of the drama group Mr. Kashikar & his wife Mrs. Kashikar. They are childless. They just make a show of love and romance by caring for each other and giving gifts to each other and that too in public. But actually Mr. Kashikar is an orthodox husband who never allows his wife to argue with him or to express her wish. Being childless, they have adopted one boy named Balu. Miss Benare ruthlessly unravels their

pettiness and plainly tells that they have adopted a boy in order to lessen the monotony of their lives. They have deprived that child of a separate identity and maturity. She says-

"- And that they shouldn't die of boredom! – gave shelter to a young boy. They educated him. Made him toil away. Made a slave out of him."

So they have adopted Balu Rokde, not out of generosity, but out of sheer need, "in order that nothing should happen to either of them in their bare, bare house – and that they shouldn't die of boredom!

Each artist of the group represents an unfulfilled dream. Boredom pervades their lives. Leela Benare describes them sarcastically which brings out the failure of the individual in this sick-hurry and divided world. About Balu Rokde she says –

"Well, we have an expert on the Law. He's such an authority on the subject, even a desperate client won't go anywhere near him! He just sits alone in the barrister's room at court, swatting flies with legal precedents! It shows Balu's failure as a barrister.

About Ponkshe – she says

"And there's a Hmm! With us sci-en-tist ! inter – failed !

So, it's clear that Ponkshe fails to become a scientist.

Tendulkar turns the opening scene of silence into a marvellous piece of satire by pitting the self-consciously independent, vehemently assertive and immensely cheerful Benare against the utterly selfish hypocritical and malicious amateur artistes who she subjects to merciless psychical dissection in order to expose their real, seamy inner selves. On hearing Mrs. Kashikar's supposed desire to buy a garland for her Benare retorts. "The garland flew away- Pouf! Or did the dicky-bird take it? I never want garlands. If I did, couldn't I afford to buy them? I earn my own living? You know. That's why I never feel like buying garlands and things."

Professor Damle's inability to be present on the occasion of the staging of the Mock Law Court "Causes many a ripple amongst the amateur artistes. Tendulkar deftly utilises this suspenseful dramatic occasion to expose the real natures of Kashikar and Sukhatme. They expose themselves through their own utterances. Kashikar's sense of social obligation, though a false one, is aroused when he says-

"How can I not worry? We owe something to the people, Sukhatme, A performance is no laughing matter."

Sukhatme is quite inefficient as a lawyer. Karnik is a failure as an actor. This petty lot finds in Benare a suitable enemy. Subha Tiwari writes

"Amongest themselves even they do not have anything but hatred for each other. Every uttering has a dual meaning for them. Even innocent remarks are taken as sexually loaded ones. These perverted people want to mentally replay the sexual encounters of Benare. They want to derive pleasure out of this crooked means".

During the mock – trial of Miss Benare, the witnesses try to show her as immoral, but actually it represents their failure in establishing relations with Miss Benare. They would like to wander freely with Miss Benare and admire before her, her intelligence, sharpness, beauty as a woman. All of them want to keep secret relations, secret enjoyment with her but no one wants to be tied down with her in a way of marriage. For life partner, they all need "ideal woman". They also feel humiliated that she has rejected them as a companion and she has established relations with Prof. Damle. All these hollow mentality becomes clearly evident in the dock of the court. Balu Rokde, as a witness reveals that once he had seen during night Miss Benare alone at Prof. Damle's house and his sudden visit astonished them. But Miss Benare reminds him the expression on her face arisen as Prof. Damle snubbed Balu in front of her as he was insulted before her. Balu, must have entertained secret love for her, but it is not materialized due to his parents. And it becomes clear when he says that while accosting Miss Benare at night, she held his hand and he gave a slap to her. By revealing this he wants to prove himself as Pure man, who is not interested in such woman. But Mr. Karnik, as a witness says that the story is different. The accused Miss Benare, asked for marriage to Rokde, but he was not ready and said

"If I marry you when you're in this condition, the whole world'll sling, mud at me. No one in my family's done a thing like that - Don't depend on me".

And Miss Benare gave him a slap. Even Ponkshe reveals that he was invited by Miss Benare in the Udipi restaurant where Miss Benare, revealed that she was pregnant and she desired to marry Mr. Ponkshe, But he rejected her. This very act of Mr. Ponkshe indicates that if he is really an ideal man he must not have accepted Miss Benare's invitation to meet her alone. If she had not revealed this he must have enjoyed a cup of coffee with her. All these witnesses reveal the pettiness of human minds. The commencement of the 'mock-trial', which constitutes a 'play-withinthe- play', offers Tendulkar ample scope to dissect and lay bare, the dormant ills of discontent in the psyche of these urban hypocrites. Though, they gang themselves up against a helpless Benare, for the time being, they have nothing but spite for one another. Kashikar, the mock – judge, banging the gaval, spitefully silences his wife "Silence must be observed while the court is in session, can't shut up at home can't shut up here! During the trial, Samant, an innocent villager, makes a passing remark "Miss Benare is really amazing". At this Ponkshe gives a deliberate twist to innocent remark "In many respects" Sukhatme, the counsel for the prosecution calls Ponkshe as his first witness in a tone soaked in sarcasm "My first witness is the world – famous scientist, Mr. Gopal Ponkshe.

They start dissecting Miss Benare's private life, - they talk about her age, the reasons for remaining single, her relations with Prof. Damle, her past affair with her maternal uncle, her attempt of suicide, her free life, her attempt to get married to give a name to her illigimate child etc. They feel pity on her and they criticize her as well. Their comments reveal that society has created very tight, rigid, suffocating rules for a woman. A woman must not be free. She must not laugh loudly. As Mrs. Kashikar says :

"Should there be no limit to how freely a woman can behave with a woman? An unmarried woman? Look how loudly she laughs! How she sings, dances, cracks jokes! And wandering alone with how many men, day in and day out."

While showing the contempt for this helpless woman, a fierce psychological violence becomes evident. The latent sadism of the characters of Sukhatme, of Mr. & Mrs. Kashikar, of Ponkshe, Karnik or even Rokde, surfaces during the process of the trial. In delineating these characters, Tendulkar has explored their psyches to the extent of revealing the hidden sense of failure pervading their lives – the inefficiency of Sukahtme as a lawyer, the childlessness of Mr. & Mrs. Kashikar, the non-fulfillment of Ponkshe's dream to become a scientist, the vain attempt of Karnik to be a successful actor and the inability of Rokde to attain an independent, adult existence.

They all try to show their power as an individual. Since they are failure as an individual they feel jealous about Miss Benare who is economically and academically very much successful and has got the reputation as a teacher. No complaint about her teaching, or being late or absent on her job. Her professional life is not stained with any blame of corruption or mal-practice or un-fair means. Whereas her group-artists are unsuccessful on professional front in one way or the other way. It is but natural that they can derive pleasure by criticizing Miss Benare's personal life which according to them is very much contrary to social norms. Only on this front they find themselves superior as compared to Miss Benare, as they are leading their lives on this ground, according to social norms, they try to establish themselves superior and try to remind Miss Benare that though she is successful woman on professional level yet she can never consider herself above over others as her personal life is stained with immorality. They try to cut her down. But as Samik Bandyopadhyay in the Introduction of "Collected Plays in Translation" rightly writes –

"It is part of Tendulkar's dramatic strategy that Benare's immediate persecutors in the play are as powerless as she, and all their exertions to cut Benare down to size are more their striving after power than a real exercise of power. As a matter of fact, Tendulkar plays at considerable length on the individual and powerlessness of each of her assailants, each of them grabbing every opportunity to expose and humiliate another, and ganging up only to attack Benare, in the process exposing their own powerlessness and their desperate need to assume a pretence of power in the collective! And yet the invisible presence of power ruling / dominating over all of them is subtly woven into the scheme with reference to the networking of forces and operations manoeuvring to throw Benare out of her job as punishment for her sin.

Mr. **N.S. Dharan** writes in **"The Tongue-in-cheek" in Silence! and Kamala"** writes –

"Samant, the innocent villager, an outsider to the rest of the group, through his utterances and actions becomes another powerful vehicle of satire against the hypocritical citywallahs. Tendulkar introduces Samant in the play not only to play a key-role in the mock-trial but also to highlight the gaping holes in the moral pretensions of his urban counterparts. On being asked by

Sukhatme to recount before the mockcourt, what he saw in professor Damle's hostel room, he with rustic innocence and ignorance replies,

"where, No, No, why that room's in Bombay! And I was in this village Hardly! It's silly – I don't know your professor Damle from Adam. How could I get to his room: isn't that right."

To quote furthur **Mr. N.S.Dharan** "The Kashikars, Balu Rokde, Sukhatme, Ponkshe and Karnik of Silence emerge as individuals belonging to the middle class who prove to be ineffectual and discontented. Their words and actions prove, beyond any doubt, that they are neurotic, sadistic, conspiratorial and even treacherous. It is not out of genuine love for drama that they have turned to theatre activity but out of a sheer sense of their own personal failures in real life. Dejected, discontented and still daring, they can only behave cruelly towards one another."

So Tendulkar, excellently satirizes the modern middle class mentality through the members of "The Sonar Moti Tenemtent (Bombay) Progressive Association" – An amateur theatre group.

6. DRAMATIC TECHNIQUES OF THE PLAY

The play has a naturalistic appearance, but being the presentation of a game, becomes an allegory where make-believe can easily blend with reality.

Mr. N.S.Dharan writes –

"Vijay Tendulkar's "Silence……, consisting of middle – class characters, is in the nature of "discussion play." The social issues discussed in it are not quite organically integrated into its plot, "but expounded in the dramatic give and take of a sustained debate among the characters. Its setting is the city and the atmosphere is tense throughout. It has three acts designed in the mode of the popular dramatic construct of the present century. There are no scene divisions of the acts."

The title itself is suggestive. Before the 'Mock-trial', Benare is active, in a sense. She makes comments on the behaviour of her fellow-characters, as well as sings. But silence descends on her when 'Mock-trial' begins with Kashikar's sudden interrogative statement – prisoner "Miss Benare, under section No 302 of the Indian Penal Code you are accused of the crime of infanticide. Are you guilty or not guilty of the aforementioned crime." Benare is dumbfounded. As the trial proceeds her attempt at protest are callously drowned in Kashikar, the Mock judge's imposition: "silence!" In such a helpless, hostile situation, Benare has no other choice but to remain Silent, as no language can come to her rescue.

The court pronouncing "Silence" itself is a mechanism to silence the natural human drive and truth under the code of the legal legitimate.

However, Banare breaks her silence at last towards the close of the play when she burst forth into long and brilliant monologue.

Samik Bandopadhyay comments,

"Benare's long monologue extends to ten minutes and to a different dramatic mode altogether, to give the play a lift from the farcic plane which it has occupied for so long, with only the occasional bursts of tension growing around Benare from time to time from point to point for departure. The Benare speech was added to the play as an afterthought when the "entire play was ready to be staged in the competition (the annual Maharashtra State Drama Competition) and it was discovered that it fell short by ten minutes of the stipulated time limits and thus was likely to be rejected by the examining panel. Tendulkar initially resisted director Arvind Deshpande's suggestion "to increase the length by ten minutes" somehow. Tendulkar about this writes –

"A woman of few words generally, came to the rescue. She suggested that the central character of the play Miss Benare, must open up somewhere, especially at the end of the last act. She could express her pent-up feelings by way of a monologue. Without Benare's articulation, the play would remain less communicative. I was of the opinion that Benare would not open up before the others in the play. That was not in her character. I refused …….. I was compelled to write. So I made Benare fly into fantasy and made her recite a prolonged Monologue."

The way the monologue is framed / presented in the play with the music "from some where in the background", the change of light and the whole court "freezing" and the sharp stylistic break in tone, the spoken is really a projection of the unspoken and naturally unheard by the other players. At the same time, Tendulkar the astute craftsman that he is, draws on a series of similar but shorter barely heard asides earlier in the play, so typical of Benare, so vulnerable and yet so determined to play her game through. The most moving of these comes in Act II, when Samant notices –

"She seems to have fallen asleep, Miss Benare, I mean"

And Benare replies –

" 'her eyes shut' – I'm awake. I can never, never sleep just when I want to. Never."

Tendulkar makes use of certain dramatic symbols in the play. The door bolt that hurts Benare's finger at the very outset, physically locks her into the hall where her tormentors persecute her. This incident in itself is an externalization of the 'no escape' plight in which she finds herself in real life. There is also the green cloth, parrot and the sad lullaby Benare sings. Both assume symbolic significance at the resolution of the play"

Structurally, the songs Tendulkar assigns to Benare are of great dramatic significance, For instance, take the song she sings in the opening scene:

> Oh, I've got a sweetheart
> Who carries all my books,
> He plays in my doll house,
> And says he likes my books.
> I'll tell you a secret –
> He wants to marry me.
> But mummy says, I'm too little
> To have such thoughts as these (SC SS-S9).

The song carries dramatic significance, as it anticipates Karnik's disclosure of Benare's fruitless love for her maternal uncle in the third Act.

The second song, a nursery-rhyme, also appears in the very same scene:

> The grass is green
> The rose is red
> The book is mine
> Till I am dead (SC 62).

The lines are again significant in that Benare realizes, in the course of the play, that she can have nothing that she can call her own.

More important than these two compositions in verse is the one which she recites in the opening scene:

> Our feet tread upon unknown
> And dangerous pathways evermore,
> ……………
> And the wound that's born to bleed
> Bleeds on for ever, faithfully
> There is a battle sometimes, where
> Defeat is destined as the end.
> Some experiences are meant
> To taste, then just to waste and spend (SC 63).

It is from the above Marathi poem by Mrs. Shirish Pai that Tendulkar has conceived Benare, the central character in Silence! In accordance with the above aphoristic kind of verse, Benare feels that she is destined to be defeated in the end.

Another ballad-like verse favoured by Benare is:

> The parrot to the sparrow said,
> 'Why, oh why are your eyes so red?'
> 'Oh, my dear friend, what shall I say?
> Someone has stolen my nest away.'
> .... (SC 74).

Benare sings it to herself towards the end of Act I and repeats it again at the end of Act III where it supposedly emerges from an indistinct source in Benare's voice. The 'parrot' in the play is suggestive of Samant and the 'nest' may refer to her chastity which she is deprived of by Professor Damle and 'the crow' too seems to be none other than the callous and selfish Professor himself.

Indeed, with the use of new dramatic devices, Tendulkar has made the drama innovative.

7. CONCLUSION

None can deny the fact that literature of every time and space springs form the cultural ethos of that time and space. The natural accordance is always to be found between the literature of a particular time, space and society of that time and space. Literature springs from culture and hence with all its aesthetics it proves to be a social and cultural document of that particular time and space. The bond between literature and culture is an everlasting phenomenon. The basic reason why this tuning is to be found between literature and the cultural ethos is the commitment of the writer. Writer experiences a greater commitment to his time and space and writes with a vision of reality as well as responsibility. His aim is to see and sees the prevailing norms of his culture in a real sense of the term and so he becomes a committed person, a committed writer. His status as a writer would be futile if there is no sense of responsibility or tone of commitment in his works. The first thing that can be concluded on the basis of the present research work on Vijay Tendulkar's plays is that he is a playwright with a conscious sense of commitment. A writer who desires to be aesthetic in his approach of writing, should in no way give himself a consent to connive at the prevailing realities of his time, culture and society. Tendulkar remains faithful not only in observing those realities but also in displaying them through his plays. He is a dramatist with commitment to his time and country. His plays are adorned with aesthetic value but he does not try to escape form his commitment. It can be justified more elaborately on the basis of his plays.

As a playwright he holds a mirror through his works before the society which is very much Indian and the society finds its own reflection in that mirror. Nothing of Society – good and evil, high and low, black and white – remains, unseen or unnoticed to him. His plays present before the spectators both the sides of life of an average Indian.

Tendulkar as a playwright reflects both the sides of Indian life – the bright side as well as the dark one. As Gouri Ramanarayan aptly observes "with his exposure to Marathi theatre form childhood and journalistic background Vijay Tendulkar turned contemporary socio-political situation into explosive drama". He has dwelt on the alienation of the modern individual, satirized contemporary politics, forcefully depicted social and individual tensions, portrayed with finesse the complexities of human character and vigorously exploited man-woman relationship in several of his works. Significantly the themes which have engaged his most frequent attention, have been the plight of woman in a maledominated urban middle class society, and the husband-wife relationship as obtained in metropolitan centers like Bombay and Delhi. Vijay Tendulkar portrays the contemporary society and the predicament of man in it with a special focus on the morbidity in his plays. His plays touch almost every aspect of human life in the modern world and share the disillusionment of the post- modern intellectuals. However, he seems to highlight three major issues: gender, power and violence.

A close study of Vijay Tendulkar's plays reveals that Tendulkar is not a teacher or preacher. He is not one of those dramatists who use their medium in the service of their favourite socio-political ideology. He is not out to propagate any particular philosophy of life. Some critics have pointed out leftist interpretation to the plays like Ghashiram Kotwal, Kamala and Sakharam Binder. It shows that his plays are open to diverse interpretations and cannot be tied down to a single line of thinking. So the question whether Tendulkar writes for life's sake or art's sake is pointless. All that we can say is that he seems to favour socialist humanism but it should also be remembered that his plays do not revolve in the orbit of that ideology either.

It is significant to note most of Tendulkar's plays are gyno-centric. He was essentially dealing with a world, which in the guise of the modern ideal of nuclear family rejected woman's independence as a citizen, enforced traditional Hindu-Brahmin norms of behavior, crushed her attempts of gaining freedom and exercised a rigid control on her sexuality and productivity.

Silence the court is in session was the first major play by Tendulkar which lodged a fierce attack on the ideology of glorification of motherhood. It also laid bare the sexual politics in patriarchal norms of family and gender relations. Miss Benare, the school teacher is a political subject in that she fiercely claims her independence as a person. It is this spirit of individualism in Benare that leads her to take a bold step of getting pregnant with the man she loves. Of course, it did not deal only with the theme of motherhood but it also exposes the asymmetrical relationship of power between husband and wife in married life and also between married women and unmarried women. Mr. Kashikar's relation with Mrs. Kashikar in the play brings out the humiliation of the typical Hindu Brahmin wife in the idolized family. It also satirizes the respectable façade of middle class men such as Kashikar, Sukhatme, Ponkshe, and Karnik. It also satirizes the value they profess. They preach the sanctity of motherhood but show absolutely no compunctions in asking Benare to destroy the foetus in her womb. So it is a play that ruthlessly exposes the lust latent in the minds of so called gentlemen.

The success or failure of any work of art depends upon its appeal – whether that appeal proves to be transitory or everlasting. A work of art with an everlasting appeal always remains eternal. It will not be out of the way or excessive exaggeration if the same thing is said about Tendulkar's plays. We do notice even today victims like Kamala, Benare, Sarita, Rama, Lalita Guari in Society. At the same time we notice even today males likes Arun, Sakharam, Ramakant and Umakant, Jaisingh Jadav, Ghashiram etc. as long as such characters are there in our society, the appeal of his plays would remain intact. His plays will never lose the quality of relevance with which they have been written.

BIBLIOGRAPHY

PRIMARY SOURCES

- **Tendulkar, Vijay** – *Collected Plays in Translation,* (Oxford University Press, 2003.)

- **Tendulkar, Vijay** – *Ghashiram Kotwal,* Seagull Books, Calcutta, 2002

SECONDARY SOURCES

- **Abrams M.H.** *"A Glossary of Literary Terms"* Macmillian. 1996

- **Abrams Teera**, *"Folk Theatre in Maharashtrian Social Development programme,"* Educational Theatre Journal 1975

- **Babu M.R.** *Political Deformity, In Indian drama Today,* Prestige - Books – 1990

- **Babu M.S.** *"Spiritual Deformity,"* In Indian Drama Today, Prestige Books – 1990.

- **Babu, Sarat M.** *"Indian Drama Today",* New Delhi, Prestige Books, 1997

- **Banerjee Arundhati**, *Introduction Five plays by Vijay Tendulkar ,* Oxford up, Bombay

- **Bhalla M. M,** *"Folk Theatre and operas",* A Handful of Dreams Kantas Book Depot, 1977, Delhi.

- **Bhasin Kamala & Khan Nighat** Said *"Some questions on Feminism and its relevance in South Asia,"* ISBN New Delhi - 1993.

- **Bhatnagar M.K.** *"Indian writings in English"* Atlantic publishers, New Delhi.

- **Bhatnagar M.K.**, *Feminist English Literature,* Atlantic Publishers New Delhi

- **Bhave Pushpa** *"Vijay Tendulkar : A Study in Contemporary Indian Theatre"*, Sangit Natak Akademi, New Delhi – 1989.

- **Bhayani Utpal** – *સામાજિક નાટક, એક નૂતન ઉન્મેષ: વિજય તેંડુલકર,* NavBharat Sahitya Mandir 1993.

- **Das Bijay Kumar** – *Critical Essay on post-colonial literature,* Atlantic Publishers.- 2001

- **Das Bijay kumar.** *"Comparative Literature,"* Atlantic Publishers, New Delhi.

- **Deshpande G.P** *"Modern Indian Drama,"* An Anthology, Sahitya Akademi, New Delhi 2002

- **Dharan N.S.** *"The plays of Vijay Tendulkar"* Creative Books – New Delhi – 1999

- **Dharan N.S.** *"The Plays of Vijay Tendulkar",* Creative Books, 1999

- **Dhawan R.K.** *"20 years of Indian writing",* IAES, New Delhi 1999.

- **Dodiya J.K. & Surendran K.V.** *"Indian English Drama, Critical Perspectives,"* Sarup & Sons – 2002

- **Gargi, Balwant.** *Theatre in India,* New York: Theatre Arts, 1962.

- **Gayle Greene and Coppelia Kahn**, *"Feminist scholarship and the Social construction of woman,"* Making a Difference : Feminist Literary criticism, London, Methuen – 1985.

- **George, K.M., ed.** *Comparative Indian Literature,* Madras: Macmillan, 1984.

- **Gowda, Anniah.** *Indian Drama,* Mysore: Univ. of Mysore, 1974.

- વઘ્રકર ભી. ન – અનુસંધાન, ગુર્જર એજન્સી, ગાંધીમાર્ગ, અમદાવાદ.

- વઘ્રકર ભી.ન. – નવોન્મેષ, ભગવતી ઓફસેટ, અમદાવાદ

- વઘ્રકર ભી. ન. – દલિત સાહિત્ય, પૂનમ ઓફસેટ, ગાંધીનગર

- **Jyenger, K.R.S.,** *Indian writing in English,* Sterling publishers – 1985. New Delhi

- **Karnad Girish** *"Author's Introduction,"* Three Plays, Oxford University press, Delhi, 1994.

- **Karnad Girish** *"Nag Mandal"* & *"Hayavadana,"* Oup – 1993.

- **Kumar, Geeta** *"Portrayal of Women in Tendulkar's Shintata Court Chalu Ahe,"* New Directions in Indian Drama. New Delhi, Prestige – 1994.

- **M. Sarat Babu** *"Vijay Tendulkar's Ghashiram Kotwal,"* A Reader's Companion, Asia book Club – New Delhi – 2003.

- **Madge V.M.-** *Vijay Tendulkar's Plays: An Anthology of Recent Criticism,* Pencraft International, 2007

- **Mehta Jay** – *Zankhi: Glimpse of Marathi Drama and Literature,* Unique offset

- **Naik M.K.** *"A History of Indian English Literature,"* Sahitya Akademi, New Delhi – 1982

- **Naik M.K. and Mokashi S. Punekar,** *Perspectives on Indian Drama in English,* Oxford UP – 1977, Madras

- **Pandey S. and Freya Barwa** – *New Directions in Indian Drama* Prestige Books.

- **Reddy, Bayapa P.** *Studies in Indian writing English with a Focus on Indian English Drama,* New Delhi: Prestige, 1990.

- **Reddy, Venkata K.** *Critical Studies in Commonwealth Literature,* New Delhi: Prestige, 1994.

- **Sarat Babu M.** – *Vijay Tendulkar's Ghashiram Kotwal,* Asia Book Club, 2003

- **Sharma Vinod Bala** *"Critical Perspectives Ghashiram Kotwal"* Asia book club- 2001.

- **Sharma Vinod Bala** *"Critical Perspectives Ghasiram Kotwal",* Asia Book Club, 2001

- **Shiply Joseph J.** *Dictionary of World Literary Terms,* New Delhi: Doaba House, 1993.

- **Srinivas M.N. ,** *Social change in Modern India,* Orient Longman – 1972

- **Surendran K.V.** *"Indian Writing : Critical perspectives Sarup & Sons."* New Delhi

- **Taraporewala Freya and Pandey Sudhakar** *"Contemparary Indian Drama,"* New Delhi, Prestige Book - 1990

- **Tendulkar Vijay** *Katha* – 2001

- **Vatsyaya, Kapila.** *Traditional Indian Theatre:* Multiple Streams, New Delhi: National Book trust, 1980.

- **Veena Noble Dass** – *"Studies in Contemporary Indian Drama,"* Prestige – 1990.

ARTICLES FROM NEWSPAPERS

- **Rajadhyaksha Mukta**, Times of India – Monday, January 29, 2007., "Times review / Book Mark., "Vijay Tendulkar answers Some questions."
- **Times News Network** "Times of India" Tuesday, May 20, 2008.
- **The Hindu** 3/10/04., The Hindu - Sunday, September 16, 2001.

WEB SOURCES

http://www.rediff.com/news/2008/may/19vijay.htm (died article)

http://www.imdb.com/name/nm0854919/ (biography)

http://en.wikipedia.org/wiki/Vijay_Tendulkar (biography)

http://www.littleindia.com/news/123/ARTICLE/3138/2008-07-15.html (By:

Shekhar Hattangadi)

http://www.hinduonnet.com/thehindu/mag/2005/11/06/stories/2005110600310500.htm (**A rich tapestry of women's stories**) Sunday, Nov 06, 2005 on kamala

http://salaamtheatre.org/kamala2004.html

www.urdutech.net/.../2008/05/vijaytendulkar.jpg

chat.indiatimes.com/articleshow/753698.cms

www.sajaforum.org/2008/05/obit-vijay-tend.html

http://news.bbc.co.uk/2/hi/south_asia/7407808.stm (death article)

www.hindu.com/.../stories/2007012002590800.htm (ghasiram) (Saturday, Jan 20, 2007)

http://www.hindu.com/mp/2007/01/20/images/2007012002590801.jpg

http://kpowerinfinity.spaces.live.com/Blog/cns!EEA9A8ECBFC1B50B!309.entry (((kanyadaan performance article) (August 11

Vijay Tendulkar's 'Kanyadaan' - An Unparalleled Performance)

www.indiaclub.com/shop/AuthorSelect.asp?Autho... (kanyadaan poster)

http://geekydood.wordpress.com/2008/04/30/silence-the-court-is-in-session/

http://www.quillandink.netfirms.com/Theatrecian/tcreview060506.htm (silence)

www.alibris.com/.../author/Tendulkar,%20Vijay (image)

http://timesofindia.indiatimes.com/articleshow/23796750.cms (article on ghasiram kotwal's performance) (30 Sep 2002, 2309)

http://picasaweb.google.com/suman.nsd/100MEDIA#5196466031138807074 (ghasiram kotwal)

http://www.mumbaitheatreguide.com/dramas/hindi/sakharam_binder_retold.asp (sakharam binder , performance article and photo)

http://www.sepiamutiny.com/sepia/archives/000636.html (photo sakharam binder)

http://www.iaac.us/Tendulkarfestival/VijayTendulkar.htm (photo with cast of sakharam binder)

http://www.bookrags.com/wiki/Shantata%21_Court_Chalu_Aahe (silence)

http://www.bookrags.com/wiki/Ghashiram_Kotwal

http://www.bookrags.com/wiki/Sakharam_Binder

http://www.bookrags.com/wiki/Vijay_Tendulkar

http://www.indianexpress.com/res/web/pIe/ie/daily/19991020/ile20071.html (article, Wednesday, October 20, 1999)

http://passionforcinema.com/a-conversation-with-sir-vijay-tendulkar/ (conversation with tendulkar)

http://shreevarma.homestead.com/bookreviews1.html

www.ingramcontent.com/pod-product-compliance
Lightning Source LLC
Chambersburg PA
CBHW071059280326
41928CB00050B/2558